All About Bottlenose Dolphins

ALL ABOUT ANIMALS ★ IN THE SEA ★

Kerrily Sapet

EZ READERS
AN IMPRINT OF MITCHELL LANE PUBLISHERS

CREATING YOUNG NONFICTION READERS

EZ Readers offer nonfiction for beginning readers in PreK through first grade, using simple language, clear illustrations, and engaging facts to build vocabulary and confidence.

TIPS FOR READING NONFICTION WITH BEGINNING READERS

Talk about Nonfiction

Begin by explaining that nonfiction books give us information that is true. The book will be organized around a specific topic or idea, and we may learn new facts through reading.

Look at the Parts

Most nonfiction books have helpful features. Our *EZ Readers* include color photographs and graphic aids, a table of contents, a glossary, and an index. Share the purpose of these features with your reader.

Color Photos and Graphic Aids

A lot of information can be found by "reading" photos, charts, maps, and other graphic aids found within nonfiction texts. Help your reader learn more about the different ways information can be displayed.

Table of Contents

Located at the front of the book, this list shows the big ideas within the text and the page numbers where they can be found.

Glossary

Located at the back of the book, the glossary defines key words and phrases that are related to the topic. These words and phrases can be found in the text in colored type.

Index

Located at the back of the book, an index is an alphabetical list of topics and the page numbers where they can be found.

With a little help and guidance about reading nonfiction, you can feel good about introducing a young reader to the world of *EZ Readers* nonfiction books.

EZ Readers is an imprint of:

Mitchell Lane
PUBLISHERS

2001 SW 31st Avenue
Hallandale, FL 33009
mitchelllanepub.com

First Edition, 2026.

Author: Kerrily Sapet
Editor: Morgan Brody

ISBN 979-8-89260-837-4 (library binding)
ISBN 979-8-90145-036-9 (paperback)
ISBN 979-8-89260-939-5 (ebook)

LC record available at https://lccn.loc.gov/2025950881

Photo credits: Shutterstock, ROMAN RYBALKO, cover, 1; Shutterstock, Northern Owl, cover, 1, 2, 3, 4, 8, 15, 19; Shutterstock, Nicolas-SB, cover, 1; Shutterstock, Disa_Anna, 3, 10, 13, 16, 18; Alamy, Mint Images, 5; Shutterstock, Geo graphics, 6, 22; Shutterstock, Nicolas-SB, 9; Shutterstock, Sokolov Alexey, 10, 22; Shutterstock, Tory Kallman, 12–13, 22; Shutterstock, Tetsuo Arada, 14, 22; Shutterstock, vkilikov, 18, 22; Shutterstock, Irina No, 20; Shutterstock, woopics, 21; Shutterstock, icemanphotos, 22; Wikimedia Commons, Esthee2010, 22

Table of Contents

Meeting an Ocean Friend 4

Dolphin Watching 8

Dolphin Families 15

Where Do Bottlenose Dolphins Live? . . . 17

Babies and the Future. 19

Parts of a Bottlenose Dolphin 21

Glossary 22

Quiz. 23

Further Reading. 24

On the Internet 24

Index. 24

About the Author. 24

Meeting an Ocean Friend

Imagine you are on a boat. The water is warm. You can see the **coast**.

Something leaps into the air. Sunlight shines on its silver-gray skin. It's a bottlenose dolphin! You are seeing one of the smartest animals in the ocean.

Dolphin Watching

The dolphin glides past the boat. It's as long as a car and weighs as much as a refrigerator. The dolphin's nose is shaped like a bottle. It swims with flippers and a tail called **flukes**.

DOLPHIN DIVE!

Dolphins are born with a small amount of hair.

You see a hole on its head. Dolphins breathe air through a **blowhole**, like you breathe through your nose. Dolphins are not fish. They are **mammals**.

The dolphin jumps.
It twists and lands on
its side. Splash! That
jump is called a **breach**.
Dolphins love to play
in waves.

DOLPHIN DIVE!

A dolphin can jump higher than a giraffe is tall.

Dolphin Families

You see more dolphins. They swim in a group called a **pod**. You look over the side of the boat. The dolphins are chasing fish and shrimp to eat.

DOLPHIN DIVE!

Dolphins play tag with each other.

Click! Squeak! You hear the dolphins making noises to call each other. Each dolphin has its own sound—like a name.

Where Do Bottlenose Dolphins Live?

DOLPHIN DIVE!

Other dolphins help take care of the calf.

Babies and the Future

You see a baby dolphin. It is called a **calf**. It is as heavy as two watermelons and as long as seven pencils. The calf drinks milk from its mother.

Bottlenose dolphins can live 40 to 60 years. **Pollution** hurts dolphins. There are about 600,000 bottlenose dolphins. They often help people in the water. Someday you might see a real bottlenose dolphin!

Parts of a Bottlenose Dolphin

Fin
A flat part on a dolphin's back that helps it balance.

Blowhole
A blowhole is a hole on top of a dolphin's head. It helps the dolphin breathe air.

Flukes
A dolphin's tail fin is two triangles called flukes.

Rostrum
A dolphin's snout that has upper and lower jaws

Flipper
A flipper is a flat paddle on a dolphin's side.

Glossary

blowhole (BLOH-hohl) the hole a dolphin uses to breathe

breach (br-EE-ch) to jump out of the water

calf (kaf) a baby dolphin

coast (KOH-st) the land next to the ocean

mammal (MAM-uhl) an animal that breathes air, has hair, and feeds its baby milk

pod (PAH-d) a group of dolphins that swims together and keeps each other safe

pollution (PRED-uh-tor) dirty air, water, or land

Quiz

1. Are dolphins fish?

A. Yes B. No

2. Do dolphins breathe air?

A. Yes B. No

3. Do dolphins eat whales?

A. Yes B. No

4. Do dolphins live in groups?

A. Yes B. No

ANSWER KEY:

1. No
2. Yes
3. No
4. Yes

Further Reading

Jeffery, Eliza. *Are Whales and Dolphins Smarter Than Humans?: Discover the Science behind Cetology.* Minneapolis, MN: Lerner Publishing Group, 2025.

Markle, Sandra. *Could You Ever Dive With Dolphins?* New York, NY: Scholastic, 2023.

Murray, Julie. *Bottlenose Dolphins.* Mankato, MN: ABDO Publishing, 2025.

On the Internet

Bottlenose Dolphins

https://kids.nationalgeographic.com/animals/mammals/facts/bottlenose-dolphin

Read more and watch a video about bottlenose dolphins.

Common Bottlenose Dolphins

https://www.montereybayaquarium.org/animals/animals-a-to-z/common-bottlenose-dolphin

Learn more and watch a supersized dolphin pod.

Dolphin Sounds

https://www.wilddolphinproject.org/our-research/dolphin-communication/

Listen to the sounds bottlenose dolphins make.

Index

blowhole 11, 21, 22
bottlenose dolphin 7, 20, 21
breach 12, 22
calf 18, 19, 22
food 15
mammal 11, 23
pod 15, 22
size 8, 19
sounds 16
tail (flukes) 8, 21

About the Author

Kerrily Sapet has written more than 30 books for kids. She lives near Chicago with her family. When she was seven, she fed a dolphin at an aquarium. She felt its smooth skin. She liked hearing its whistles, squeaks, and clicks. Sapet has seen dolphins at the beach in New Jersey and Florida. She hopes to see more dolphins someday.